New Vanguard • 13

Scorpion Reconnaissance Vehicle 1972–94

Christopher Foss & Simon Dunstan • Illustrated by Peter Sarson

First published in Great Britain in 1995 by Osprey Publishing,
Midland House, West Way, Botley, Oxford OX2 0PH, UK
44-02 23rd St, Suite 219, Long Island City, NY 11101, USA
E-mail: info@ospreypublishing.com

Transferred to digital print on demand 2010

First published 1995
2nd impression 2005

Printed and bound by PrintOnDemand-Worldwide.com, Peterborough, UK

A CIP catalogue record for this book is available from the British Library

ISBN: 978 1 85532 390 2

Filmset in Great Britain

Acknowledgements
DRAC, The CO 1st The Queen's Dragoon Guards, The CO The Light Dragoons, The CO The Queen's Royal Lancers, Alvis Vehicles Ltd,
Bob Beadsmoore, Colonel (Retd) Charles Delamein, Ken Fletcher, Lieutenant-Colonel (Retd), George Forty OBE, Jason Grainger,
Captain J M Holtby, The Household Cavalry Regiment Museum, Tim Neate, Lieutenant-Colonel (Retd), Michael Norman, P Info UKLF,
RAC Tank Museum, Soldier Magazine, Jenny Spencer-Smith, Robin Watt, Martin Wickham.

In Memoriam
W F D

FOR A CATALOGUE OF ALL BOOKS PUBLISHED BY OSPREY
MILITARY AND AVIATION PLEASE CONTACT:

Osprey Direct, c/o Random House Distribution Center,
400 Hahn Road, Westminster, MD 21157
Email: uscustomerservice@ospreypublishing.com

Osprey Direct, The Book Service Ltd, Distribution Centre,
Colchester Road, Frating Green, Colchester, Essex, CO7 7DW
E-mail: customerservice@ospreypublishing.com

www.ospreypublishing.com

SCORPION CVR (T)

DESIGN AND DEVELOPMENT

'Time spent on reconnaissance is rarely wasted' is a military axiom that has stood the test of time in the unceasing quest to see over 'the other side of the hill'. The role of reconnaissance troops is to discover the dispositions of the enemy and discern his intentions while relaying this information to the force commander. Within armoured forces, there are two schools of thought as to the most appropriate method to gain this intelligence – by force or by stealth. The former approach requires a well armed and armoured vehicle capable of fighting opposing tanks on almost equal terms while the latter a smaller, highly agile vehicle which possesses superior surveillance equipment but only sufficient firepower for self-defence. It is a function of each doctrine that has a profound effect on the design of an Armoured Fighting Vehicle (AFV) for reconnaissance purposes.

Early Reconnaissance Vehicle

The British Army has traditionally advocated reconnaissance by stealth. At the outbreak of World War 2, the divisional reconnaissance regiments of the BEF were equipped with machine gun armed Light Tanks together with Bren and Scout Carriers. As the war progressed and it acquired global dimensions, the British Army employed numerous types of vehicles from the contemporary Cruiser tank, the A27 Cromwell, in the Armoured Reconnaissance Regiments of the Armoured Divisions, to the diminutive Daimler Dingo Scout Car which served in almost every formation in the army. From El Alamein to Arnhem and from Caen to Kohima, a gamut of wheeled and tracked vehicles was pressed into service in the reconnaissance role while at the war's end, a plethora of prototypes was leaving the

The commander and gunner of a Scorpion of 1 Troop, A Squadron, 14th/20th King's Hussars, scan the horizon during Exercise 'Glory Hawk' in October 1973 in the Harz Mountains north of the Moselle valley in Scorpion's first major exercise in West Germany. The first regiments in BAOR to be equipped with Scorpion were 17th/21st Lancers and 14th/20th King's Hussars at Wolfenbüttel and Herford respectively; hence the combined name of 'Glory Hawk' from the Death or Glory motto of the Lancers and the Hawk insignia of the Hussars. Note the damage to the smoke grenade bin on the turret side. (MoD)

designer's drawing boards, several of them featuring multi-wheel configurations and mounting the same 75mm main armament as fitted to the majority of Allied gun tanks in the West; a tacit admission that reconnaissance vehicles must have greater firepower for self-defence.

In the years after the war, many of these wheeled armoured cars proved invaluable in policing the far-flung British Empire and in the 'brush-fire' wars that characterized the 1950s and 1960s. Although Cromwell tanks remained in the reconnaissance troops of armoured regiments well into the 1950s, it became almost an article of faith in the British Army as to the necessity of wheeled AFVs for reconnaissance. This was reflected in the first armoured cars fielded to replace the wartime designs – the FV700 series 4x4 Ferret for close reconnaissance in 1952 and FV600 series 6x6 Saladin for medium reconnaissance in 1959. A companion vehicle to Saladin was the 6x6 Saracen Armoured Personnel Carrier (APC) introduced earlier in 1953 to meet the urgent need for armoured transport for the infantry in the Malayan Emergency to counter communist insurgents.

These vehicles proved highly successful in service but, by the early 1960s, Britain's extensive overseas commitments were proving too costly and to maintain permanent garrisons around the world became a prohibitive drain on defence resources. As an alternative strategy, it was proposed that troops were to be transported by air from Europe to trouble-spots around the world in the newly acquired long-range transport aircraft, such as Argosy, Belfast and, later, Hercules, before heavy armour and reinforcements arrived by sea. To support the airlanded contingent, an AFV capable of providing fire support and with an anti-armour capability was necessary, while, at the same time, itself being airportable.

Meanwhile, with the Saladin now in service, the British General Staff began considerations for its successor and discussions began at the Fighting Vehicles Research and Development Establishment (FVRDE) at Chertsey near Chobham in Surrey as to whether a practicable design could combine the requirements for a reconnaissance vehicle capable of undertaking its role during general warfare in Europe while being light enough to be airportable.

Development of the AVR
In 1960, design work began on the Armoured Vehicle Reconnaissance (AVR) which was to mount a 76mm or 105mm gun in a limited traverse turret housing the three-man crew including the driver. The gun for fire support was complemented by a separate compartment at the rear containing Swingfire Anti-Tank Guided Weapons (ATGW) to provide the anti-armour capability. The design addressed both tracked and wheeled configurations and it shared the same Rolls - Royce K60 engine and the Allison transmission of the contemporary FV432 APC and the FV433 Abbot 105mm self-propelled gun. This ambitious and complex proposal, however, resulted in a projected combat weight of over 13 tons which far exceeded the airportability limit.

Simultaneously with the design of the AVR, FVRDE was investigating a number of other concepts and technological innovations during the early 1960s. Among these was a compact self-propelled gun carriage with a dismountable 105mm howitzer for the Royal Artillery, the Lightweight Close Support Weapon System, which featured a chassis with four wheel stations per side and introduced the concept of the driver being seated beside a front mounted engine and transmission.

Although the Royal Artillery did not accept the design, the proposed chassis was used as the basis for a family of Lightweight High Mobility Tracked Vehicles that would be truly airportable, with any three being carried in an Argosy transport aircraft. At a maximum weight of 4.5 tons, there were four variants in the family including a 120mm recoilless rifle weapon carrier; a reconnaissance detachment carrier; a two-stretcher ambulance and an anti-APC infantry support carrier. Other essential requirements included high automotive performance with low ground pressure and the ability to cross inland waterways and rivers without preparation.

The AVR Design
It was apparent that there would have to be a significant reduction in weight if the vehicles were to be airportable while providing more than a modicum of protection against small arms fire and artillery fragments. Among the technological advances at this time was the use of aluminium alloy armour for AFVs; the first to be produced in quantity being the M113 APC in 1959 by FMC of San Jose, California. The armour of the M113 consists of the 5083-type aluminium-magnesium-manganese alloy which is relatively easy to weld but the weight per unit area it protects is almost identical to that of steel armour. But as the aluminium armour plate is thicker than steel armour, it has greater structural rigidity thus obviating the need for as many cross members and stiffeners as used in previous light, steel armoured AFVs. This both reduces overall weight and simplifies manufacture while increasing internal volume for other components, as well as enhancing bouyancy as compared to a steel vehicle. Further research also revealed that aluminium armour gave superior protection against fragment attack such as artillery splinters because of its greater areal density. Overall, significant reductions in weight could be realized in compact AFVs through the use of aluminium armour.

During Exercise 'Glory Hawk', one Scorpion of 17th/21st Lancers was detached to give a demonstration of its capabilities to the West German defence minister. On its return, the Scorpion was passing the famous Nürnburgring circuit where, on Sundays for the price of 7DM, members of the public can drive their private vehicles around the race track. Following the conclusion of Exercise 'Glory Hawk', a race was organized between Scorpions of the Hussars and the Lancers; it ended in a dead heat. (MoD)

Since its introduction into service, the weight of the FV700 series Ferret armoured car had risen from 3.5 to almost 5 tons and more power was desirable in order to maintain its required mobility. In 1964, a standard Jaguar XK 4.2 litre petrol engine was fitted in place of the original Rolls-Royce B60. Extensive trials over 50,000 miles were undertaken without major failure which proved that the Jaguar engine could perform reliably in a wheeled AFV.

All these factors were considered by the Concepts Section at FVRDE and it was decided to build an experimental vehicle designated TV15000 in order to test many of these technical features. Designed and built in 1965, the TV15000 made extensive use of aluminium in its construction and incorporated hydropneumatic suspension units which in the event provided little better performance over torsion bars for the extra cost, weight and complexity incurred. An extra wheel station was soon added to the four per side of the original design to improve cross-country mobility. At the outset, the TV15000 was powered by a Rolls-Royce B60 engine with a gross output of 130 bhp but following the successful trial in Ferret it was replaced by the Jaguar engine in

1966 which gave a considerable increase in power. This coupled with specially developed lightweight aluminium tracklinks allowed the TV15000 to travel at over 50 mph (80 kph) – speeds unheard of for AFVs since the days of Walter Christie's innovative tanks designs of the 1930s. Both tracked and wheeled solutions were still being considered at this time; the latter being a six-wheeled vehicle with skid-steering which in the event proved to be too large to meet the design parameters.

The CVR(T) Series

During this period, the General Staff and the Royal Armoured Corps had refined the requirements for the next generation reconnaissance vehicle despite a joint collaborative venture with Australia, Canada and the United States to produce an Armoured Reconnaissance Scout Vehicle which would be adopted by each nation. Design work on the project began at FMC in 1964 but no mutual agreement could be reached by the four parties and it was abandoned in October 1965.

Mindful that the weight of the AVR had spiralled due to the number of roles required of it, the General Staff decided in April 1965 to

develop a family of two complementary vehicles – one armed with a 76mm gun in a fully-rotating turret for fire support and one fitted with Swingfire ATGW launchers for engaging and destroying heavy armour at long ranges while both were to be capable of acting as reconnaissance vehicles. To this end the RAC requested a higher level of armour protection which was needed for high intensity warfare in Europe than had been envisaged for the Lightweight High Mobility Tracked Vehicle family. Accordingly the weight limitation was raised to 17,500 lb which would allow two such vehicles to be carried in a Lockheed C-130 Hercules in the airlanding role or one if it was to be airdropped by parachute.

The weight limitation of 17,500 lb became immutable throughout the design phase of what was now known as the Combat Vehicle Reconnaissance (CVR). Another stringent parameter was the width of the vehicle which was not to exceed 84in. It has been stated that this stipulation was made so that the vehicle could negotiate between trees in Malaysian rubber plantations which are supposedly seven feet apart or the width of a fully laden elephant. But the reason is far more prosaic; it is the maximum width of equipment permitted by Unites States Air Force regulations for carriage in the back of a Hercules while allowing the loadmaster enough space and time (in an emergency) to escape down the side of

The CVR(T) was first used operationally by the British Army in 1974 when The Blues and Royals deployed their Scorpions to Heathrow airport as a counter to terrorist threats against certain international airlines. These two 'cars' standing guard during Operation 'Trustee' with a Metropolitan policeman in the turret show several features of early Scorpions. Of interest, the nearer Scorpion has a 'blast guard' over the forward portion of the stowed floatation screen – one of the earliest Scorpion modifications after its entry into service; and fitted as standard during manufacture from vehicle No.60. (MoD)

the vehicle when set for airdrop by parachute.

Furthermore, the General Staff required the CVR to be as quiet as possible, to be able to swim and be able to negotiate soft ground, necessitating a ground pressure of approximately 5 psi or about the same as a marching soldier. Finally, the General Staff determined that the two vehicle family be expanded by a further four variants; an APC; an ambulance; a command post and a recovery vehicle. All these models together with the ATGW launcher version required a superstructure at the rear for their various functions which established the basic configuration of CVR with the engine, transmission and driving compartment in the front. This common layout simplified production and therefore reduced manufacturing costs.

Since the width and weight were fixed, the overall dimensions of the vehicle were virtually determined because the ratio of the length of the

A prototype Scorpion, recognisable by the additional pair of headlights fitted with IR filters, undergoes wading trials to test its amphibious capability. The collapsible rubberised floatation screen of CVR(T) can be erected in under ten minutes and allows the vehicle to negotiate still rivers and waterways at speeds of up to 3.6 mph (6 km/h) while the generous freeboard of this system allows even steep-sided river banks to be negotiated on entry and exit. (Alvis)

tracks on the ground to the distance between the track centres is fixed within strict limits by steering considerations. This dictates that, to suit the steering ratio and the desired ground pressure, the tracks had to be about 18in. wide, leaving 4ft. for the hull width. As 2ft. of space is the minimum required for a driver fitted out in Arctic clothing, only 2ft. was left for the engine compartment.*

This had serious implications in the choice of an engine for CVR which would have to be significantly more compact than the engines then in use if the required power to weight ratio of 25 bhp/ton was to be met. Although the desirability of a diesel engine was realized for its torque characteristics, range advantages and reduced fire risk, the calculated weight penalty of over 500 lb was too great for air-portability. Only one British engine fitted all the requirements and this was the 4.2 litre Jaguar engine, since no special tank engine could be developed before the proposed in service date for CVR of 1971.

With the design parameters substantially set, FVRDE was authorized to build two test rigs. These essentially comprised the front hull section of CVR in order to check the efficiency of the

cooling system; traditionally a weak point in British AFV design. Indeed, the first installation with its complicated drive system of twin centrifugal fans proved to be both costly and unreliable. A new development by Airscrew Howden of a single mixed flow fan gave the same performance as the twin fan configuration but was far simpler to install whilst reducing overall power requirements.

Meanwhile the second test rig was fitted out as a Mobile Test Rig to test the automotive features of CVR, in particular the suspension and transmission. By now the series was designated the Combat Vehicle Reconnaissance (Tracked) or CVR(T) to differentiate it from the proposed successor to Ferret, Combat Vehicle Reconnaissance (Wheeled), which was subsequently named Fox. Following the examples of Saladin and Saracen, CVR(T) was named beginning with S, with the 76 mm fire support version being Scorpion because its rear mounted turret suggested a sting in the tail. The others clearly reflected their function: Striker with its ATGW; Spartan as the APC; Samaritan as the armoured ambulance; Sultan as the command post and Samson as the recovery vehicle. In addition, the General Staff had identified the need for a seventh member of the family which was to be another turreted vehicle armed with a 30 mm high velocity cannon to conduct

* To be exact the stipulated space required for a 90 percentile man is 25.16 inches (639mm) and as the actual track width is 17 inches (432mm) to which must be added clearance, plus two times the armour thickness of the hull plates, the internal width of the hull is 45.25 inches (1149mm).

close reconnaissance. This variant was called Scimitar. In its original design configuration, the commander of CVR(T) was to act as gunner but after User pressure, following a feasibility study codenamed 'Cayuse' at the Royal Military College Shrivenham which indicated that his work load would be too great, this was changed to commander/loader.

The FV721 Fox

While the Scorpion family fulfilled the British Army requirement for CVR(T), that for the Combat Vehicle Reconnaissance (Wheeled) was met by the FV721 Fox. A total of 15 prototypes of FV721 was built by Daimler Ltd between November 1967 and April 1969 and Fox was accepted for service by the British Army in July 1970. The 4x4 Fox has a three-man crew comprising commander, gunner and driver and is fitted with a two-man turret armed with the same 30 mm Rarden cannon and 7.62 mm co-axial machine gun (MG) as Scimitar. Production of Fox was undertaken by the Royal Ordnance Factory Leeds with Alvis providing the turrets. As a liaison vehicle, Ferret was to have been replaced by another version of Fox called Vixen but this was cancelled in the defence cuts of 1972.

Trials and Production

In September 1967, Alvis Ltd of Coventry was awarded a development contract to produce 30 prototypes of CVR(T). P1-P17 were Scorpion while P18-P30 were of the other six CVR(T) variants. Following its extensive experience in building the Saladin armoured car and its derivatives, Alvis undertook detail design work for the complete series using innovative manufacturing techniques and proven commercial components wherever possible in order to meet the strict cost limitations imposed by the Ministry of Defence. Completed on 23 January 1969, the first prototype was delivered on schedule; within budget and at the specified weight: a remarkable triple achievement in the development of any AFV.

There followed extensive testing across the globe with hot weather trials being conducted in Australia and Abu Dhabi, and cold in Canada and

A pair of Scimitars and the companion vehicle to the CVR(T) series, the Combat Vehicle Reconnaissance (Wheeled) Fox engage targets on the RAC gunnery ranges at Lulworth in Dorset with their 30mm Rarden cannons. First deployed in 1975 with 1st Royal Tank Regiment, Fox did not prove as successful as its illustrious forerunner the Ferret and never actually superseded it in service. (Simon Dunstan)

With its turret traversed to the rear to aid stability and avoid damage to stowage bins from the strops, a prototype Scorpion dangles beneath a US Marine Corps CH-53 Sea Stallion during airlifting trials. One of the fundamental design parameters of CVR(T) was airportability by C-130 and comparable transport planes. The advent of heavy lift helicopters such as the CH-53 and, latterly medium lift helicopters (such as late model Chinooks) has greatly enhanced the airportability of the complete CVR(T) family which range in weight from the originally specified 17,500 lb of Scorpion to over 19,000 of Sultan and Samson. (Alvis)

Norway to prove that the vehicle could operate in extremes of conditions and temperatures of -25°F (-32°C) to +125°F (+52°C). A prototype Scorpion was also pressure tested in the British Aircraft Corporation stratosphere chamber at Weybridge in Surrey to determine power losses at altitude. CVR(T) was formally accepted for service with the British Army in May 1970 and a production contract was awarded to Alvis on 30 July 1970 for 275 Scorpion and 288 Scimitar vehicles. The first production Scorpion was completed in 1971 and first deliveries to the British Army began in January 1972. The last CVR(T) vehicle in a total of 1,863 for the UK Ministry of Defence was delivered in 1986 with a breakdown by type as follows:

Scorpion	313
Striker	89
Spartan	691
Samaritan	50
Sultan	291
Samson	95
Scimitar	334

At the height of production in the mid 1970s, 40 CVR(T) were built a month at the Alvis factories in Coventry.

TECHNICAL DESCRIPTION

The FV101 Combat Vehicle Reconnaissance (Tracked) Scorpion is a compact, highly mobile, airportable light tank. Designed primarily for battlefield reconnaissance, it is also capable of undertaking numerous other roles such as fire support to infantry; counter-insurgency; road and cross-country convoy escort; force flank protection; route marking and the ever increasing demands for internal security ranging from patrolling airport perimeters to counter international terrorism to peacekeeping duties as part of a United Nations protection force.

Entering service with the British Army in early 1972, Scorpion superseded the Saladin 6x6 armoured car in the medium reconnaissance role but the latter was to continue in service for many years undertaking internal security and peacekeeping duties in areas where tracked vehicles are deemed politically unacceptable. Armed with the L5A1 76mm gun, Saladin weighs 25,536 lb (11607 kg) with a three man crew whereas Scorpion with the L23 gun of the same calibre and a similar

number of crew weighs only 17,500 lb (7940 kg). But much of this reduction in weight has been achieved by the compact configuration of Scorpion which means less room inside for the crew as compared with Saladin. All members of the CVR(T) family share common automotive components; suspension and basic layout, which has significant procurement, training and logistic advantages.

Sgt 'Sandy' Sandbrooke keeps watch from the turret of his Scorpion of 3 Troop, A Squadron, 16th/5th The Queen's Royal Lancers, on the perimeter of the British Sovereign Base Area at Dhekelia during the Turkish invasion of Cyprus in August 1974. This was the first occasion that Scorpions were deployed by C-130 in the airportable role to protect British interests overseas. (MoD)

Driving the CVR(T)

The driving compartment is situated in the front to the left of the engine with the combined transmission and steering unit in the nose of the vehicle. The driver has an adjustable seat with a folding backrest to allow access into the turret; either as a means of escape in an emergency or as access to the turret to use the commode beneath the commander's seat when operating under NBC conditions; a procedure fraught with difficulty. For a urinal the crew was also provided with an interesting device known as the 'Beresford funnel'. Tucked in the hull sponson to the driver's left is the main instrument panel which makes it difficult to be seen when driving with his head out. The driver steers the vehicle using tillers and gear changing is done with the left foot similar to the method used on motorcycles. Originally the method was to change up by moving the pedal

With a bridge classification of 10 tons each, three Scorpions of 'C' Squadron, 16th/5th The Queen's Royal Lancers, cross a Class 60 Medium Girder Bridge built by 68 Gurkha Field Squadron at Sek Kong in October 1974. Well suited to the difficult and diverse terrain in Hong Kong, Scorpions replaced the Centurion MBTs which were too heavy and unwieldy as armoured support to the colony's garrison. (MoD)

upward with the toes and to change down by downwards pressure with the foot. However, when wearing full NBC protection clothing with its cumbersome galoshes it was possible to jam a foot between the gear change pedal and the brake so a simpler heel and toe pedal was introduced. There is a single wide angle periscope for driving whilst closed down which can be replaced by a Pilkington passive image intensification periscope for driving at night.

The Engine
The CVR(T) series is powered by the Jaguar J.60 4.2 litre, six-cylinder, overhead valve, spark ignition engine with a single Marcus carburettor and a compression ratio reduced from 9.1 to 7.75:1 to run on military grades of petrol which also reduces its gross output from 265 bhp to 195 bhp at 5,000 rpm. With a combat weight of 7.8 tons, this results in a power to weight ratio of 24.32 bhp per ton (17.85 k/tonne) at a nominal ground pressure of 5psi (0.35 kg/cm2) giving both high

acceleration and agility while enabling Scorpion to negotiate soft ground impassable to most other tracked vehicles of its generation. The maximum speed is approximately 50 mph (80 kph) and an acceleration from rest to 30 mph (48 km/h) in 16 seconds is possible. All members of the family were fitted with a collapsible floatation screen around the top of the hull. This could be erected in under ten minutes and the vehicle could then propel and steer itself across rivers and lakes using its tracks at a maximum speed of 3.6 mph (6.5 km/h).

TN15X Transmission
The drive from the engine is transmitted through a centrifugal clutch, thereby eliminating the need for a clutch pedal, to the Merrit-Wilson TN15X transmission designed by Self Changing Gears. Derived from the design used in Chieftain, the TN15X comprises a semi-automatic, hot-shift, epicyclic gearbox with seven speeds, in both forwards and reverse. It also incorporates a triple differential steering system which is controlled by hydraulically applied disc brakes operated by the driver's tillers. The radii of turns differ with the gear ratio selected and a facility for pivot turn is incorporated. Although relatively simple to drive for a tracked vehicle, Scorpion does have its foibles; particularly when changing down from fourth gear to third because, in the hands of an

inexperienced driver, the vehicle tends to nose dive sharply much to the discomfort of the turret crew. The single epicyclic reduction gear final drives transmit power to the front mounted sprockets where some 70 per cent of the engine power is available indicating the high efficiency of the system. For engine cooling, a single 12in. (305mm) mixed flow fan by Airscrew Howden draws in air through the radiator over the transmission, then over the engine and out through the louvres above the engine.

CVR(T) is mounted on a transverse trailing arm torsion bar suspension system with five twin aluminium road wheels on each side. Dampers are fitted on the front and rear wheel stations with a vertical wheel movement of 11.8in. (0.3m) which gives a comparatively comfortable ride across open country, but its short track length on the ground inhibits high speeds across broken terrain. With a width of 17in. (432mm), the lightweight steel

An Army Air Corps Gazelle helicopter of the Force Reconnaissance Unit comes into land behind a Scimitar of 'C' Squadron, The Life Guards, during exercise 'Hardfall' in February 1977 – the annual British Army winter work-up exercise in Norway before participating as part of Allied Command Europe (ACE) Mobile Force (Land) in the NATO combined Exercise 'Avalanche Express' above the Arctic Circle. To suit the theatre of operations, the black stripes of the standard black and green camouflage scheme are overpainted with white paint while the registration number, national insignia and unit serial indicator are masked with tape during application. (MoD)

tracks have rubber pads on both the road and road wheel sides to minimise noise, but track clatter is pronounced and Scorpion can often be heard at a considerable distance. Track life depends on a number of factors including terrain and maintenance but typically is around 3,000 miles (4800 km) of mixed road and cross-country running. All a credit to its design.

A prototype Spartan poses for a company publicity photograph at the Alvis test track in Coventry in mid 1971. This vehicle is fitted with the ZB298 battlefield surveillance radar made by Marconi Avionics Ltd. This equipment was one of the first of its kind and could only be used when the vehicle was stationary. One hundred units were procured for use with Spartan but it required a skilled operator to differentiate between different types of moving objects in the field and there was rarely sufficient training on the equipment to bring operators up to scratch so it did not last long in service. (Alvis)

FIREPOWER

The fighting compartment of Scorpion is located at the rear of the hull in a fully rotating turret with the commander on the left and the gunner on the right. Between them is the L23A1 medium velocity 76mm gun which, through the use of higher tensile strength steel, is some 25 per cent lighter than the L5A1 version installed in the Saladin armoured car. Simple, reliable and robust, the L23A1 is an effective weapon which above all merits the accolade of being 'soldier proof'. Forty rounds of 76mm ammunition are carried in a mix of HESH (High Explosive Squash Head); HE; Smoke; Illuminating and Canister; a typical ammunition load being 15 HESH; 20 HE and five Smoke with Illuminating rounds being carried for night operations. The L29 HESH round is the primary round for defeating medium armour, but it is also highly effective against buildings; concrete emplacements and other battlefield targets whilst its lethality against troops in the open or under light cover is only marginally less than conventional HE.

The main armament of the Scorpion has a maximum elevation of 35° and a depression of 10° throughout the full range of turret traverse. To save cost and weight, the gun controls and turret traverse are manually operated which is one of the most unpopular aspects of Scorpion with its crews. A clinometer and traverse indicator are fitted as standard. Secondary armament is a 7.62mm L43A1 GPMG mounted co-axially to the left of the 76mm gun. Three thousand rounds of 7.62mm ammunition are carried and, in addition to being used in the normal suppressive fire role, the L43A1 can be used as a ranging gun for the main armament out to 1100m, although this technique is not taught in the British Army where the 'Eyeball Mark I' is the standard method of range estimation for direct fire. With the extended range graticule fitted to the gunner's sight, indirect fire out to 7000m is possible. Being such a light vehicle, Scorpion is prone to 'platform rock' when firing to the front so crews tend to fire the main armament either at 11 or one o'clock to the hull axis to reduce this effect; one o'clock being preferred because there is less heat shimmer in the gunner's sight from the cooling air outlet louvres. Similarly, both the commander and gunner either press their faces firmly into their sights or else lean their heads well back to obviate the fierce recoil on firing. Failure to do so can result in condition known as 'Scorpion nose' when the hard rubber eyepiece of the sight strikes the bridge of the nose causing a pair of black eyes.

Observation Systems

As befits a reconnaissance vehicle, Scorpion incorporates a comprehensive array of optical sights for

A wire-guided Swingfire anti-tank missile leaps from the launcher bin of a CVR(T) Striker of 171 (The Broken Wheel) Battery of 32 Guided Weapons Regiment, Royal Artillery, during training on the ranges at Larkhill in September 1978. Striker is the first purpose-designed anti-tank guided weapon vehicle to be deployed with the British Army. The first production Striker was delivered in June 1975 and it entered service with the Royal Horse Artillery in BAOR in 1976. (MoD)

Sergeant Mouse directs his Scorpion of 'C' Squadron, 16th/5th The Queen's Royal Lancers, from an LCT of HMS Intrepid during a beach landing exercises at Lulworth in 1981 – the year that wading screens were removed from CVR(T). This Scorpion and Scimitar are assigned to ACE Mobile Force (Land) and are painted in the yellow and green camouflage scheme applied for service on the southern flanks of NATO in either Greece or Turkey. Both these vehicles have been fitted with the 7-in. headlights of Ferret and Saladin in place of the 5-in. Sealed beam units which proved to be less durable. (MoD)

the commnder and gunner. The latter also has an L3A1 Image Intensification (II) night sight made by Rank Precision Industries. Scorpion is the first production AFV to have passive night vision equipment for driving, surveillance and gunlaying but there is no provision for the commander. While the II sight is effective during hours of darkness, it is less so in rain or mist. Furthermore, the phosphor green image causes eye strain after approximately 30 minutes so the gunner and commander usually swap positions when on OP duty. A further problem when acting as an OP during cold nights on exercise is condensation forming on the eyepieces from the crew's breath; a piece of clean cotton rag being an essential item in the turret. The problem becomes even worse if the BV (Boiling Vessel) is in use. Nevertheless, the observation and gunnery system of Scorpion was highly effective in its day and a major advance over many of its contemporaries.

Communication systems

However good the observation devices may be it is essential that the information obtained on reconnaissance be relayed promptly to the higher com-

mand. Efficient communications are therefore vital and Scorpion has a combination of VHF and HF radio sets for short and longer range communications respectively. Originally fitted with Larkspur radios, the standard communication system for CVR(T) comprises the Clansman VRC 353, 321 and 322 sets which are installed in the turret bustle. A Nuclear, Biological and Chemical (NBC) filtration system of the overpressure type is provided to protect the crew from contamination. Mounted on each side of the forward part of the turret is a bank of three electrically operated smoke grenade dischargers to produce a smoke screen behind which the Scorpion can retreat to cover in an emergency.

PROTECTION

Scorpion is the first all-aluminium AFV to be produced in quantity in the UK but its principal form of protection is its compact size and agility so that it remains a difficult target to detect and engage. All the variants are of all welded construction using an improved aluminium-zinc-mag-

nesium AA7017-type of alloy fabricated to the Alcan E74S specification, with rolled plate, extrusions, castings or forgings being used in construction as appropriate. The armour provides protection over the frontal arc against 12.7mm (0.50 inch) rounds and against 7.62mm (0.30in.) elsewhere – the 12.7mm calibre being that of the standard Soviet AFV-mounted heavy machine gun. All aspect protection is afforded against shell fragments from High Explosive (HE) 105mm rounds, either ground or air burst, at over 33 yards (30 m) distance. The hull configuration is designed to lessen mine blast and additional armour plate is welded to the floor of the driver's compartment to give him extra protection.

However, the innovative use of aluminium armour did present problems in subsequent years when a condition known as Stress Corrosion Cracking became apparent in the late 1970s. The effect was caused by variations in the microstructure of the armour plate during manufacture. At

A Spartan of 1st Royal Tank Regiment drives down a country road during Exercise 'Royal Reynard' in West Germany during 1979. Spartan entered service with the British Army in April 1978 and was originally intended as the replacement for the Saracen APC which, however, was to soldier on for many years; notably for internal security duties in Northern Ireland where tracked vehicles are deemed politically to be unacceptable. (MoD)

its worst, visible cracks appeared in the armour which did little to enhance the crews' faith in their vehicles – it being most serious in the gun mantlets of Scimitars which were subsequently fabricated by alternative means. After extensive research at the Military Vehicles Experimental Establishment (formerly FVRDE) at Chertsey, a remedial programme codenamed Exercise 'Scorepole' was initiated during 1978 which restored CVR(T) to serviceable condition. Subsequently strict quality control in manufacture of an improved 7017 alloy configured to MVEE 1318B specification, with additional controls on its

Acting in its classic role as the eyes and ears for the MBTs of the armoured regiments, a Scimitar of 16th/5th, The Queen's Royal Lancers, keeps a look-out during an FTX in Germany in 1979. Above and to the left of the co-axial MG is the ejection port for spent cases from the 30mm Rarden cannon. On the turret side is the early issue PVC hold-all which rarely survived long on FTXs, being ripped by trees and spilling the crew's possessions. They preferred the Chieftain metal stowage bins; as here fixed to the turret side behind the PVC hold-all. (MoD)

fabrications has virtually eliminated the problem.

Scorpion was hurried into service early in 1972 in order to forestall the possibility of cancellation in the expected cuts from the Defence Budget which occurred later in the year; the fate that befell the Vixen liaison vehicle. Accordingly several components, notably the gunner's image intensification night sight, were not fully developed before production began and others had not been tested to the usual thorough degree. As a result, several niggling problems, particularly with the gearbox, arose in the early years but, with increasing user experience and continued research by Alvis, most of these were rectified during a base overhaul modification programme codenamed Exercise 'Bargepole' which began during 1975-76. In all, some 600 Post-Design Services modifications have been applied to CVR(T) during its career but nearly all have been of a minor nature; the most significant being the aforementioned Scimitar gun mantlet and latterly the adoption of Messier hydraulic suspension dampers in place of the original Armstrong type which had been designed for a Leyland bus. It is a tribute to the designers that so few and essentially minor modifications have had to be made to CVR(T) in its 20 odd years of service.

Following the Argentinian invasion of the Falkland Islands on 2 April 1982, a Task Force was assembled, including two Medium Reconnaissance Troops drawn from 'B' Squadron of The Blues and Royals based at Windsor, and was despatched to the South Atlantic four days later. Here, with the regimental flag flying from the turret, Scorpion Two Three Alpha advances into Port Stanley with troops of 2nd Battalion, The Parachute Regiment, on 14 June 1982. (Household Cavalry Regiment via Alvis)

THE CVR(T) IN BRITISH SERVICE

When the CVR(T) series was introduced into British Service, the Royal Armoured Corps fielded eight armoured reconnaissance regiments and 11 armoured regiments, including a training regiment. The Army's major commitment to the North Atlantic Treaty Organization was 1 British Corps stationed in Germany as part of the Northern Army Group. From 1975, 1(BR) Corps was organised into four armoured divisions, each with one Type A armoured reconnaissance regiment; two armoured regiments and three mechanised infantry battalions. Each reconnaissance regiment included one close reconnaissance squadron with five troops of eight Scimitars; these troops were attached to the division's armoured and infantry battle groups to provide an integral close reconnaissance force. Under the direct control of the reconnaissance regiment commander

were two medium reconnaissance squadrons; each comprising four troops of four Scorpions and a survey troop of five Spartans, equipped with ZB298 ground surveillance radar. In the four Type B armoured reconnaissance regiments, one stationed in Germany and three in the UK, the five troops of the close reconnaissance squadrons were equipped with six CVR(W) Foxes in place of Scimitars. From its entry into service in 1978 until 1981, Striker equipped the anti-tank batteries of the Royal Horse Artillery, one of which was allocated to each armoured division.

Reorganisation of CVR(T)

The 1981 reorganisation of 1(BR) Corps into three larger armoured divisions affected the employment of the CVR(T) series. Of the five reconnaissance regiments based in Germany, three were converted to armoured regiments and the remaining two were converted to corps reconnaissance regiments, equipped with 48 Scimitar, 16 Spartan and 16 Striker vehicles. Each regiment had four identical squadrons comprising a headquarters with two

Besides the British Army, CVR(T) is also employed by the Royal Air Force for airfield defence. In November 1981, the RAF Regiment took delivery at Catterick of its first Scorpion from an order of 184 Scorpions and variants. Here, 'Rock Apes' of No.1 Squadron, RAF Regiment, patrol the perimeter of a Harrier Force deployment on Sennelager Training Area in 1987. (Simon Dunstan)

The Sultan is an Armoured Command Vehicle employed in large numbers by the British Army as mobile control posts for commanders from squadron level upwards in virtually every formation on the battlefield. Here, two Sultans of the Rgt.HQ 13th/18th Royal Hussars, are de-ployed for directing staff during an exercise on Salisbury Plain. They are parked back-to-back to allow a penthouse to be erected for greater working area under cover, providing protection against the elements. (Tim Neate)

Sultan ACVs; three reconnaissance troops with four Scimitars; a guided weapons troop with four Strikers, and a support troop with four Spartans. To compensate for the loss of the divisional reconnaissance regiments, the 13 mechanised infantry battalions received a reconnaissance platoon of eight Scimitars, while the 14 armoured regiments were each established for a reconnaissance troop of eight Scorpions.

The three regular armoured reconnaissance regiments equipped with the CVR(T) series in the UK were also reorganised. Two regiments had NATO roles, one with the 3rd Armoured Division based in Germany and the other with the UK Mobile Force; a reinforced infantry brigade ear-marked to bolster Denmark's defences in time of war. The latter regiment also provided a squadron and a Striker troop to the multi-national Allied Command Europe Mobile Force (Land). The armoured reconnaissance regiments in BAOR had three medium reconnaissance squadrons, each with four troops of two Scorpions and two Scimitars; a guided weapons troop of four Strikers, and a support troop of five Spartans. The Life Guards and The Blues and Royals, in rotation, provided the armoured element which was assigned to 5th Airborne Brigade in the home defence and out-of-area roles. This regiment had two reconnaissance squadrons equipped with the CVR(W) Fox and a tracked squadron with four

troops, with two Scorpions and two Scimitars, and a support troop with five Spartans. Members of the support troop in all regiments were trained in dismounted patrolling; demolitions and laser target marking. The three regiments based in the UK, in turn, provided a CVR(T) troop for the British garrison in the former Central American colony of Belize until its withdrawal in 1994.

The terrain in the Tactical Area of Responsibility of the British Forces in Bosnia ranges from lush and verdant valleys to bleak and barren mountains such as that shown here in January 1994 with a Scimitar of 'C' Squadron, The Light Dragoons, guarding The Redoubt, a Royal Engineers' position at the highest point on Route Triangle which is a section of the Main Supply Route from the port of Split into Central Bosnia. (MoD P.Info UKLF)

Falklands War 1982

The CVR(T) was the first to see combat service with the British Army during the 1982 Falklands War when The Blues and Royals provided 3 and 4 Troops from 'B' Squadron for the task force which recaptured the Falkland Islands from the Argentinians. Both troops, each consisting of two Scorpions and two Scimitars, with a Samson in support, landed with the assault troops and dug in to await the expected Argentinian counterattack. The main opposition to the landing came from the Argentinian Air Force which mounted numerous determined air attacks, during one of which a Scimitar claimed to have used its 30mm Rarden cannon to destroy an A-4 Skyhawk fighter-bomber. When 5th Infantry Brigade landed on 1 May, 3 and 4 Troops were ordered to join the brigade in the area of Fitzroy; the move expected to take two days was accomplished in only six hours.

On 11/12 June the Scorpions used their 76mm guns firing HESH to support the successful night assault on Mount Longdon by 3rd Battalion The Parachute Regiment. On the night of 13/14 June

Samaritan is the armoured ambulance variant of the CVR(T) family and is designed primarily for casualty evacuation from forward battle areas. The first prototype was completed in 1973 with the first production vehicles being delivered in 1978. Here, callsign Fourteen Bravo, a Samaritan of Squadron Headquarters, 'B' Squadron, The Light Dragoons, provides medical cover during Operation 'Cabinet' on 19 May 1993 when a major UNHCR convoy from Belgrade was escorted by The Light Dragoons over the Bosnia/Serbia border. (MoD P.Info UKLF)

3 Troop supported the attack by 2 PARA on Wireless Ridge while 4 Troop provided fire support to the assault on Mount Tumbledown by 2nd Battalion Scots Guards. Before the main attack, 4 Troop joined a Scots Guard patrol to stage a diversionary attack; no contact was made until the troop leader's Scorpion struck a mine. Although the vehicle was disabled, no crew member was injured beyond temporary deafness and the troop leader moved to another vehicle to direct the fire of his troop. Both attacks were successful and the next day the Argentinian commander surrendered. During the campaign the vehicles covered an average of 560 km over difficult, boggy terrain, with only one gearbox change required. The Scorpions fired an average of 60 76mm rounds while the Scimitars fired about 120 30mm rounds each.

Gulf War 1991

The massed armour battle for which the British Army had been training since 1949 occurred not in West Germany but in the Middle East when a US led coalition liberated Kuwait from Iraqi occupation in February 1991. The British contribution to the ground battle, the 25,000 strong 1st (British) Armoured Division, included a medium reconnaissance regiment, 16th/5th The Queen's

Royal Lancers (16/5L), with a fourth squadron from 1st The Queen's Dragoon Guards (QDG) attached. The design of the CVR(T) series was based upon the British Army's principle of reconnaissance by stealth. The featureless desert terrain, which allowed virtually unlimited visibility in good weather, made the traditional employment of the lightly armoured vehicles impracticable particularly as the CVR(T) was slower than the Challenger 1 MBT moving across country. Moreover, during operations at night and in poor visibility, the Challenger 1, with its superior Thermal Observation and Gunnery System, was able to observe and acquire targets at much longer ranges than the Scorpions and Scimitars which were equipped with first generation image intensification sights.

Accordingly, 16/5L was placed under operational control of Commander Royal Artillery (CRA) who grouped them with 32nd Heavy Regiment (12 M110A2 203mm self-propelled howitzers) and 39th Heavy Regiment (12 Multiple Launch Rocket Systems) to form a General Support/Recce Strike Group (also known as the Depth Fire Group) to conduct the depth battle. For this new role, 16/5L was supported by 73 Observation Post Battery (from 32 Hy Regt) with four OP parties, one attached to each squadron,

and three Forward Air Controllers to direct the 75 US Air Force A-10 and F-16 sorties expected to be allocated to CRA each day. The regiment also had in direct support 49 Field Battery, with the battery commander and his party attached to regimental headquarters.

For the advance to target 16/5L generally moved on two axes with a frontage of five kilometres; speed out of contact varied from 20 kilometres an hour in daylight to 10 kilometres at night. By midnight on 25 February (G+1), the regiment had advanced 80 kilometres into Iraq with no enemy contact other than Iraqi soldiers seeking to surrender. At first light on 26 February, 'B' Squadron 16/5L and 'A' Squadron QDG were identifying enemy positions on Objective LEAD, an Iraqi reinforced mechanised battalion, before the attack by 7th Armoured Brigade later that day; MLRS strikes began at 0647 and were soon joined by A-10 sorties. While still directing air and artillery strikes, all four squadrons were soon involved in direct fire engagements with the enemy in a confusing battle. After losing several T-55s to Swingfire missiles fired by Striker at long ranges, an Iraqi armoured column abandoned its attempt to reinforce the Iraqi forces on Objective LEAD. After this successful action, the Depth Fire Group's assets were split between 4th

A Scimitar of B Squadron, The Light Dragoons, accompanied by a pair of FV432 APCs, acts as an Observation Post (OP) overlooking Brcko in July 1993; the scene of some of the most intense fighting on account of its commanding position at the narrowest point of the Posavina Corridor which is strategically vital to the Serbians. Such OPs are of great importance for intelligence gathering about the dispositions of the various factions. Information of the shifting frontlines can be transmitted by satellite to the negotiating tables in Geneva in just 30 minutes to provide real time intelligence to the participants in the protracted peace talks. (MoD P.Info UKLF)

and 7th Armoured Brigades and A Squadron QDG was tasked to lead 7th Armoured Brigade's advance into Kuwait. With the division now deep into Iraq, the three squadrons of 16th/5L were tasked to provide rear area security for the division's combat service support tail. With the Iraqi army routed the war ended on 28 February.

The nature of the terrain, combined with the speed of the advance, made close reconnaissance by the Scorpion troops and Scimitar platoons of the armoured and infantry battle groups difficult. These sub-units were better employed for flank protection and route marking as well as providing protection for battle group headquarters and service support echelons. The infantry battle groups of 4th Armoured Brigade, which had only a single armoured regiment, sometimes operated without

One of the CVR(T)'s major tasks is to clear airfields of unexploded ordnance following an aerial attack of RAF airfields and bases. To this end, RAF EOD (Operations) Flights are equipped with Scimitars and Spartans, such as this one at RAF Mount Pleasant on East Falklands where EOD operations will continue for many years. Note the armoured cover to the NBC filter pack on the hull side and the RAF Bomb Disposal insignia on the front hull plate. This vehicle is missing its rubber dust flaps at the front revealing the metal stiffeners with their U-shaped cutouts which stop the rubber dust flaps when fitted from being abraded by the tracks and rapidly wearing out. (Tim Neate)

any Challenger 1 squadrons attached. In 3rd Battalion Royal Regiment of Fusiliers Battle Group, a reconnaissance group was formed by combining the reconnaissance platoon; elements of the anti-tank platoon including the four Spartan MCTs; an artillery forward observation officer and mortar fire controller, and supporting engineer and fitter sections. The group, with its powerful anti-tank component, was capable of independent action and destroyed a large enemy position on the night of 26 February.

The Javelin air defence missile batteries, mounted in Spartan, of 12 Air Defence Regiment found themselves in 7th Armoured Brigade being employed in the combined role of air and ground defence for which the Spartan was well suited. To provide a hasty blocking capability, 21 Engineer Regiment was equipped with four Stormers mounting the Vehicle Launched Scatterable Mine System (VLSMS), but there was no occasion to use them in earnest.

Operation 'Grapple' Bosnia
In October 1992, the British government committed an armoured infantry battle group to the United Nations Protection Force in Bosnia-Hercegovina. Armoured reconnaissance squadrons equipped with CVR(T) have been provided in turn by 9th/12th Royal Lancers and The Light Dragoons. In March 1994, a second infantry battle group, including an additional armoured reconnaissance squadron was deployed. The light, agile Scimitar has proved to be well suited to escorting aid convoys along difficult mountain roads, as well as many other tasks in support of UN humanitarian operations.

MODIFICATIONS & VARIANTS

Under the 1991 'Options for Change' defence reorganisation, the regular army's 14 armoured and five armoured reconnaissance regiments have been reduced to eight armoured; one training and two armoured reconnaissance regiments. In place of 1(BR) Corps, the UK now contributes 1st (UK) Armoured Division to the defence of Germany and 3rd (UK) Division, based in the UK, to NATO's Allied Command Europe Rapid

Scimitar, 3 Tp., 'B' Sqn, Blues & Royals, East Falklands, June 1982

A

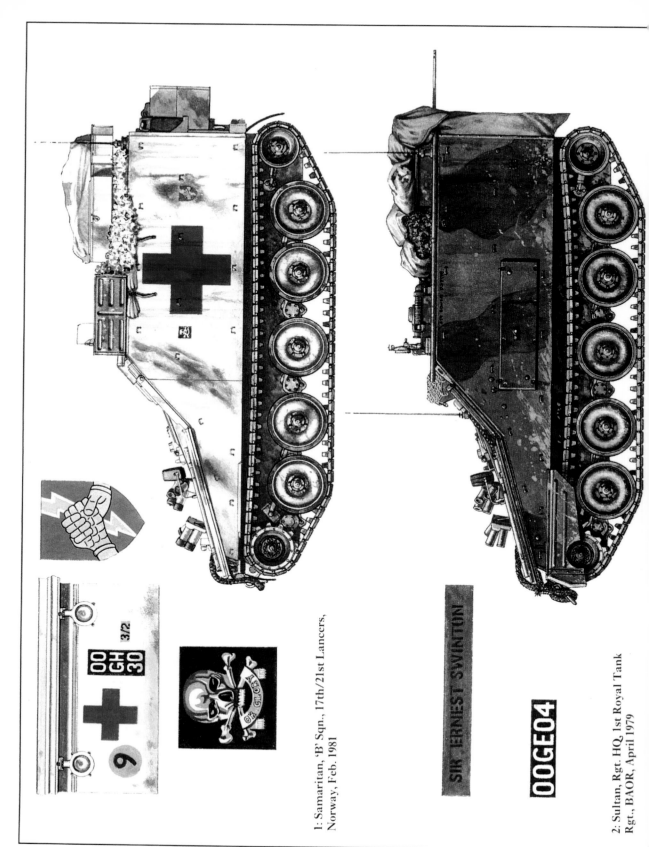

1: Samaritan, 'B' Sqn., 17th/21st Lancers, Norway, Feb. 1981

SIR ERNEST SWINTON

00GE04

2: Sultan, Rgt. HQ, 1st Royal Tank Rgt., BAOR, April 1979

B

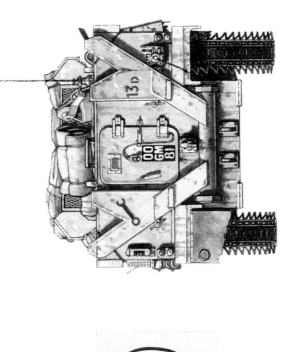

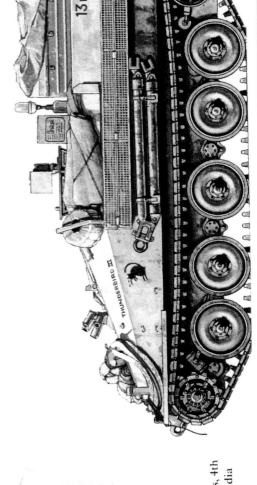

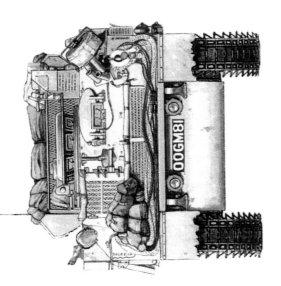

FV106 Samson, 14th/20th King's Hussars, 4th Armoured Bde. Operation 'Granby', Saudia Arabia, December 1990

FV101 SCORPION

D Squadron, 13th/18th Royal Hussars (PMO), Ace Mobile Force (Land), NATO Southern Contingent, Tidworth, 1990

SPECIFICATIONS

Crew: 3
Battle weight: 7.8 tons
Length: 14ft. 4.75 in
Height: 6ft. 10 1/2 in
Ground clearance: 1ft. 2 in
Engine: Jaguar 4.2 litre Gasoline, 2 OHC Military Version, 6-cylinder
Power/ weight ratio: 24.96 bhp/ ton
Full capacity: 88 gallons
Ground pressure: 5 lb/ sq in
Max speed: 50 mph
Acceleration: 0-30 mph in 16 seconds
Braking distance: 50 ft from 30 mph
Fuel consumption: 5 miles/ gal at 30 mph
Range: over 370 miles
Obstacle clearance: 20 in
Trench crossing: 6.75 ft
Fording: 3 ft 6 in (without floatation screen)
Water speed: 4 mph (tracks), 6 mph (propellers)
Gearbox: TN 15Z Crossdrive, semi-automatic 7-speed
Main armament: 76 mm L23 gun
Elevation: +35° to -10°
Range: 3.1 miles (indirect fire), 1.35 miles (direct fire)
Ammunition: 40 rounds (HE, HESH, HE&SH/ Practice, smoke cannister and illuminating)
Secondary armament: Coaxial 7.62mm GPMG (3,000 rounds)
Smoke dischargers: 2 triple barreled, 18 grenades also carried
Radio sets: Types C42/B47 or C13/B47 or C13/42 or Clansman

KEY

1. Transmission Breather
2. Engine Air Intake
3. Fan Bulkhead
4. Generator
5. Battery Breather
6. Jaguar 4.2L Engine
7. Air Filter (Engine Air)
8. Cooling Air Outlet Louvres
9. Driver's Periscope
10. 7.62mm Machine Gun
11. 76mm Main Armament
12. Night Sight Balance Weight (Fitted in lieu of night sight)
13. Multi Barrelled Smoke Dischargers
14. Gunner's Night Sight
15. Traverse Indicator
16. Commander's Sight Mounting Ring
16. Turnbuckle: Sight Linkage
17. Gunner's Sight
18. Turret Services Box
19. Antenna Tuning Unit
20. Intecom Control Box
21. Gun Guard
22. Gunner's Hatch
23. Glasnman Radio F/T
24. Commander's Hatch
25. Radio Antenna
26. Unity Vision Periscope
27. Stowage Bins
28. Flotation Screen Platform (Screen Deleted)
29. Idler Wheel
30. Commander's Seat (and Commode)
31. Rady Round Stowage
32. Interior Light
33. Engine Bay Fire Ext (Piped to Compartment)
34. Driver's NBC Air Outlet
36. Gear Indicator
37. Electrical Fuses
38. Steering Tillers
39. Damper Linage
40. Drive Sprocket
41. Bump Stop
42. Gear Change Pedal
43. Central Warning Light
44. Radiator Trunnion
45. Generator Panel
46. Engine/Driver B'Head
47. Radiator
48. Recovery Eyes

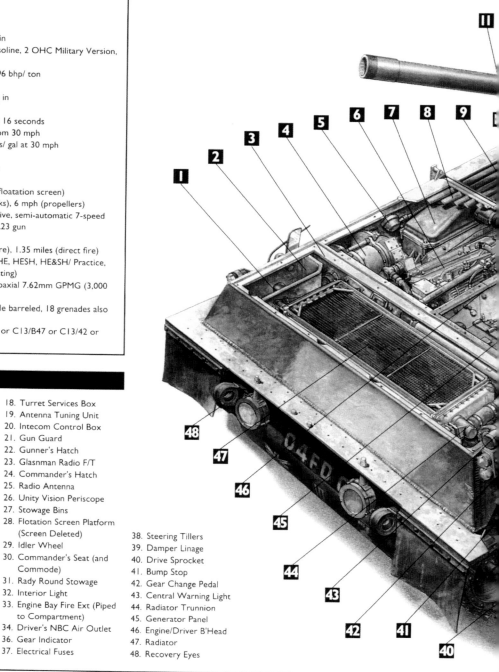

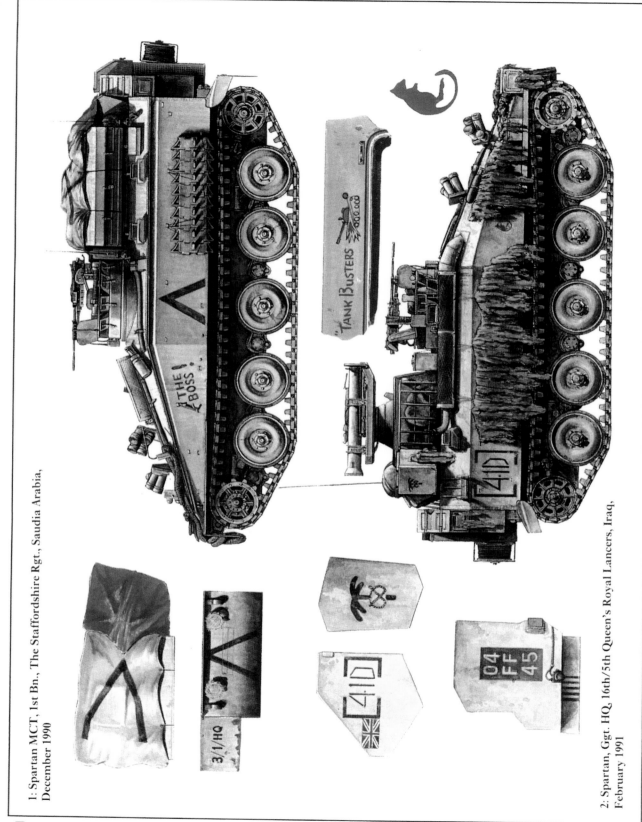

1: Spartan MCT, 1st Bn., The Staffordshire Rgt., Saudia Arabia, December 1990

2: Spartan, Sgt. HQ, 16th/5th Queen's Royal Lancers, Iraq, February 1991

E

Striker, Guided Weapons Tp., 'A' Sqn., 1st
Queen's Dragoon Guards, Feb. 1991

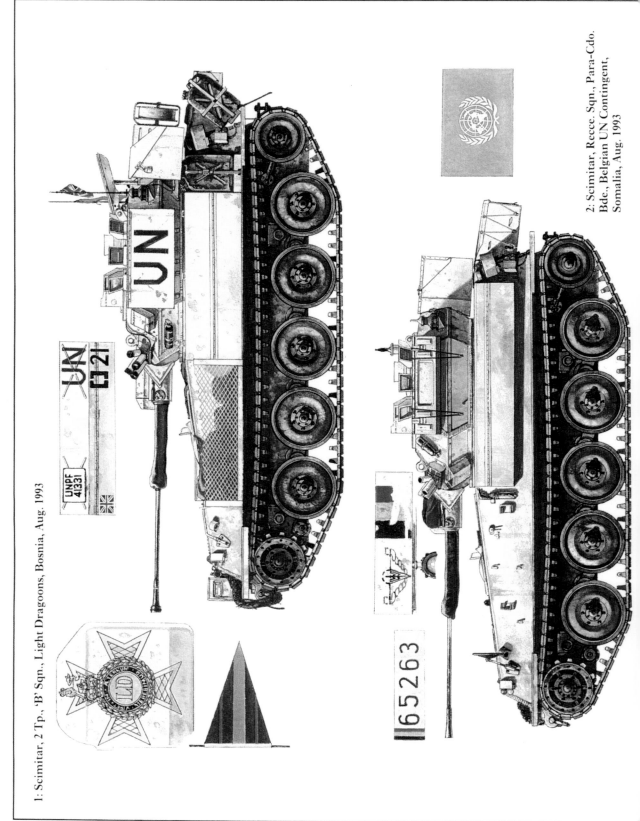

1: Scimitar, 2 Tp., 'B' Sqn., Light Dragoons, Bosnia, Aug. 1993

2: Scimitar, Recce. Sqn., Para-Cdo. Bde., Belgian UN Contingent, Somalia, Aug. 1993

An essential vehicle to support any formation using CVR(T) is the Samson Armoured Recovery Vehicle (ARV) which can effect recovery of all members of the range as well as carry out frontline repairs in the field. The vehicle is manned by the Royal Electrical and Mechanical Engineers (REME). With a REME pennant flying at the radio antenna, a Samson ARV of the fitter's section in the Reconnaissance Troop of the Royal Scots Dragoon Guards waits for a call to come to the aid of any disabled vehicles during an exercise on Salisbury Plain. Note the oversized rearview mirrors, characteristic of Samsons, to allow the driver better rearward vision when towing a casualty. (Tim Neate)

Reaction Corps (ARRC). One reconnaissance regiment, The Light Dragoons, is now based in Germany while the Household Cavalry Regiment (HCR) based at Windsor is assigned to 3rd (UK) Division. To support 5 Airborne Brigade, part of 3rd (UK) Division, an HCR squadron is designated 'Air Squadron' with the majority of its personnel being parachute trained. The Queen's Own Yeomanry, a Territorial regiment to be equipped with Sabre reconnaissance vehicles, is also committed to the ARRC.

During the course of Operation 'Granby', Alvis Vehicles Limited proposed a series of modifications for the CVR(T) vehicles deployed to the Gulf of which the most important were the fitting of Messier dampers to improve cross country mobility and an enhanced armour package that would add one ton to the vehicle weight. In the event, few of these modifications were implemented but CVR(T) performed creditably during Operation 'Desert Storm' despite its age although certain limitations did become apparent. The most serious of these was the inferior performance of its first-generation image intensification night sight as compared to the thermal imaging sights of Challenger and Warrior. The situation was somewhat ameliorated by the mounting of the Optical and Thermal Imaging Sight (OTIS) above the commander's periscope of CVR(T) but OTIS can only really be used while the vehicle is stationary and with the commander exposed which is not satisfactory during battle.

Tracer

In 1992, a replacement for CVR(T) was approved with the promulgation of Staff Target (Land) 4061 for the Tactical Reconnaissance Armoured Combat Equipment Requirement or TRACER with a proposed First Off Production (FOP) date of the year 2004. Accordingly, CVR(T) must continue in service into the 21st century by which time many of the vehicles will be over 30 years old. In 1993 it was decided to rationalise the British Army's disparate fleet of reconnaissance vehicles and several famous names were selected to be withdrawn from the inventory including Saladin, Ferret, Scorpion and Fox. With the demise of the 76mm calibre, the L21 30mm Rarden cannon has become the standard main armament for the remaining reconnaissance vehicles of the British Army with the attendant advantages of standardization with Warrior. However as many of the Scorpions and

A Spartan of 'C' Squadron, The Light Dragoons, acts as a checkpoint near Zepce in March 1994. Because of its less aggressive appearance than Scimitar or Warrior, Spartan enjoys more flexibility of movement in disputed areas, being employed for numerous tasks such as the movement of casualties or VIPs. Note that this Spartan has the larger Samson-type rearview mirrors. A common modification to CVR(T) in Bosnia is the fitting of a metal stanchion above the hull or turret to cut wires strewn across the road that otherwise could decapitate the crew members. (MoD P.Info UKLF)

Foxes to be phased out of service were perfectly sound it was decided to marry the hull of Scorpion with the turret of Fox to produce a vehicle with much the same characteristics as Scimitar. The design work and construction of two prototypes was undertaken by Alvis Vehicles Ltd and it was accepted for service with the British Army as the Sabre. During 1994-95, 104 Scorpion vehicles are being converted to Sabres at the Base Ordnance Depot Donnington.

In order that CVR(T) can continue to perform effectively in operational service until the advent of TRACER, a Life Extension Programme (LEP) is being implemented. Known irreverently within the Royal Armoured Corps as the 'Zimmer Frame Programme', the three major aspects of LEP include the replacement of the Jaguar J60 petrol engine by a more fuel efficient diesel one with its reduced fire risk and increased range; the installation of a secure communications system to enhance the Clansman VRC 353 radios and a Thermal Imaging (TI) sight under armour to overcome the deficiencies of OTIS. A new 30 mm anti-armour (Armour Piercing Enhanced Performance) is also being introduced. It has been proposed that the TI sight for CVR(T) will use

some elements from the TOGS (Thermal Observation and Gunnery System) equipment salvaged from Chieftain MBTs that have been withdrawn from service. This will allow simultaneous and independent use by the commander and gunner for both observation and gunlaying. Other improvements under consideration include the installation of a laser rangefinder to increase first round hit probability and a Global Positioning System navigation aid as used in the Gulf War. Once all these improvements have been completed in 1997, CVR(T) will remain a highly effective vehicle into the next century.

PLATES

Plate A: *FV107 Scimitar, 3 Troop, 'B' Squadron, The Blues and Royals (RHG/D), Operation 'Corporate', East Falklands, JUNE 1982*

The vehicle is finished in the standard British Army temperate zone camouflage scheme of black stripes over the green base colour. The callsign 23C is painted in white on a black square on the

This Spartan MCT of the Royal Irish Rangers, the Demonstration Battalion at the School of Infantry at Warminster, sports an interesting variation of the black over green camouflage scheme during an exercise on Salisbury Plain.

right-hand side of the turret rear bin. On the rear hull plate is the vehicle registration plate 06FD97; that on the front hull plate has been painted over for security purposes. Similarly, the vehicle bridging plate has been painted over as being redundant in the Falklands. On the lower rear hull plate is the black and white bars of the convoy distance marker. Scimitars of the Blues and Royals customarily bear the regimental insignia on the gun mantlet beside the 30-mm Rarden cartridge case ejection port but this was also painted out prior to landing for security purposes. On the turret side is the 'B' Squadron insignia stencilled in red and on the lower front turret side is the movements information code painted on all ACE Mobile Force vehicles and those committed to 'out-of-theatre' operations; painted in white capital letters one above the other is CHALK FAW RAW AUP. When deployed by RAF C-130 Hercules, the relevant information is chalked or painted beside each letter group to aid RAF 'movers'. CHALK denotes the aircraft and order for the vehicle to be carried; FAW is the Forward Axle Weight; RAW is the Rear Axle Weight and AUP is the All Up Weight. Being deployed by ship during Operation 'Corporate', no chalk marks appear on this vehi-

cle. Two Three Charlie, being the junior callsign within the troop, had the distinction of being the first CVR(T) to land at San Carlos, having motored through the shallows for 200 metres from landing craft to shoreline. Commanded by Lance Corporal of Horse J C Fisher, it was also the first CVR(T) to fire on targets in Port Stanley and finished the campaign with a 'well-filled game book'.

Plate B1: *FV104 Samaritan, 'B' Squadron, 17th/21st Lancers, Ace Mobile Force (Land), Exercise 'Hardfall', Norway, February 1981*
The vehicles of AMF(L) deployed to the Northern flanks of NATO are normally painted in white stripes over the black of the temperate zone camouflage scheme but this Samaritan has been painted white overall with green patches sprayed on top. 00GE30 is applied front and rear. Below the latter is the convoy distance marker. Bridging classification is a black 9 on a solid grey circle on the lower hull front is the unit identification serial 3/2. On all quarters are distinctive Red Crosses as befits an ambulance together with one on the cover of the top stowage bin to indicate the vehicle's function to aircraft. On the forward face of this bin on the right hand side (as viewed from

the front of the vehicle) is the insignia of ACE Mobile Force. This marking is also applied behind the Red Cross on the left hand hull side only while forward of the Red Cross is the silver on black skull and crossbones regimental motto of the 17th/21st Lancers - hence its nickname amongst other units of 'Boneheads'. When deployed on operations in Norway, old CVR(T) hands often adjust the torsion bars in their splined housings to raise the suspension by a couple of inches in the belief that it gives better floatation over snow - note the difference in vehicle height as compared to Sultan in Plate B1 with its correct track tension of a gap of one hand (four inches) or a cigarette packet between the track and the centre roadwheel. Typical of vehicles deployed to Norway, the commander has a polycarbonate screen forward of his cupola to reduce the wind-chill factor. Similarly, drivers often fit a metal shroud over the engine air outlet louvres to deflect warm air over their faces when driving 'head out'. In 'high rise' variants of CVR(T), (Sultan, Samaritan, Spartan and Samson), there is just room enough to slot a water jerrycan inside the hull under the outlet louvres so that there is a supply of warm water for the essential brew of tea when halted; water jerrycans carried externally are often frozen solid in this area of operations. Of note, crews do not usually apply camouflage stripes to roadwheels because, when travelling at any speed, the stroboscopic effect engendered makes the vehicle readily visible at a distance.

Plate B2: *FV105 Sultan, Regimental Head-quarters, 1st Royal Tank Regiment, Exercise 'Royal Reynard', BAOR, April 1979*
This Sultan Armoured Command Vehicle depicts the simple camouflage and markings scheme applied to British Army vehicles in BAOR of black stripes over a base colour of green. The vehicle registration number 00GE04 is carried on the front and at the bottom of the rear door,

below which is the convoy distance marker with its illuminating lamp above. The only other marking is the name SIR ERNEST SWINTON, one of the original tank designers, painted in black capital letters along the top of the left hand hull side. This Sultan has the original issue fibre glass trackshrouds which aided propulsion during floatation; however they did not last for any length of time on exercise so they were usually removed and only fitted for parades. However they were popular with drivers because they were more effective at reducing the amount of dust being thrown up into their faces than the simple rubber flaps that are normally fitted to CVR(T).

Plate C: *FV106 Samson, Fitters Section, 14th/20th King's Hussars, 4th Armoured Brigade, Operation 'Granby', Saudi Arabia,*

The registration 00GM81 is painted on the lower

Throughout its life CVR(T) has been progressively improved by Alvis (now Alvis Vehicles Limited) while retaining the essential characteristics of the original concept. Many of the developments embodied in the latest models have been the direct result of operational experience, notably the Falklands and Gulf campaigns. Such are the improvements in firepower and automotive performance that the family of vehicles is now known as Scorpion 2 (formerly Scorpion 90). Designed primarily for the export market, Scorpion 2 is fitted with a modified turret mounting a Cockerill Mark 3 90mm gun which can fire a wide range of ammunition. (Alvis)

hull front and on the rear door of the winch compartment. On the arms of the earth anchor attached to the rear hull is a graphic depiction of a spanner similar to the military map symbol for recovery units and the callsign Thirteen Delta which is repeated on the right hull side beneath the exhaust shroud and on the gun plank holder on the left hand side. Similarly, the Black Jerboa of 4th Armoured Brigade is emblazoned on each

Above;
The shortcomings of Spartan as an APC prompted Alvis to produce an enlarged design capable of carrying a section of 11 infantrymen and their battle equipment. First produced in 1981, the vehicle is named Stormer and forms the basis for a family of vehicles capable of being tailored to numerous roles on the battlefield. In 1986, Stormer was selected by the British Army as the carrier platform for the Shorts Starstreak High Velocity Missile System (HVM). This has a power operated turret with eight Starstreak Surface-to-Air Missiles that are ready to launch with additional missiles being carried internally. Powered by a Perkins T6-3544 diesel engine, the Stormer HVM and its companion vehicle, the Troop Reconnaissance Vehicle (TRV) which acts as both a missile resupply vehicle and OP, are to enter service with the British Army in 1995. (Tim Neate)

Above right;
The largest user of CVR(T) after the British has been the Belgian Army. Following a Memorandum of Understanding between Britain and Belgium to share development costs of CVR(T), the first of seven contracts was signed in June 1971 for a total of 701 Scorpions and variants which were assembled from 'knocked-down kits' supplied by Alvis at a British Leyland facility at Malines/Mechem in Belgium with the last vehicle being delivered in November 1980. During the Cold War, 1st Belgian Corps was assigned to NATO's Northern Army Group and included three reconnaissance battalions; 1e Jagers te Paard, 2e Jagers te Paard and 4e Chasseurs à Cheval, each equipped with 72 CVR(T). Here, a Scimitar and a Scorpion of 2e Jagers te Paard halt at the roadside during an exercise in Germany in 1979. (Pierre Touzin)

hull side. On the left hand sloping face of the hull beside the driver is the vehicle name THUNDERBIRD III in black - a reference to the children's TV puppet programme; while on the opposite side is the alternative vehicle name

Rescue Rangers in more ambitious script from another children's TV programme, the cartoon Chip N' Dale. The black object draped over the front of the Samson is an inter-vehicle starting cable together with a Marlow nylon kinetic energy

Right;
As part of the Stormer family, there is a flatbed variant similar to Streaker but, having six roadwheels per side, is capable of carrying greater payloads. The first prototype of the Stormer High Mobility Load Carrier was completed in 1989. It can be configured to undertake numerous tasks including the carriage of stores such as ammunition pallets and fuel bowsers as well as the GIAT Industries Minotaur mine scattering system. (GIAT Industries)

tow rope which is capable of recovering bogged vehicles of up to 30 tons.

Plate D: *FV101 Scorpion, D Squadron, 13th/18th Royal Hussars (pmo), Ace Mobile Force (land), Nato Southern Contingent Role, Tidworth, 1990*

Finished in the green over base yellow camouflage scheme characteristic of CVR(T) deployed to Greece and Turkey as part of Allied Command

The drivers of two Sultan ACVs of Regimental Headquarters, Royal Scots Dragoon Guards, catch some sleep during an exercise prior to Operation 'Desert Sabre'. Typical of vehicles in the Gulf, the vehicles are festooned with external stowage including

the much prized folding sleeping beds, purloined or bartered for from US Forces personnel, hanging from the nearer vehicle in the elasticated stowage netting that is a standard internal item for all variants of CVR(T) and Warrior IFV.
(Tim Neate)

Left;
As part of Britain's commitment to defend Belize against aggression, a reinforced troop of CVR(T) has served in the former Central American colony since 1976. Acting as 'armoured support' to the resident British Army infantry battalion and to the Belize Defence Force, the Scorpions and Scimitars conduct patrols throughout the country, enjoying the freedom of unrestricted track mileage, over all manner of terrain; from mountain tracks and

jungle paths to the sandy shores of the Caribbean. Here, 02FD89 (one of the original Scorpions to be deployed to Belize) of Alimal Troop, 16th/5th The Queen's Royal Lancers (note the regimental 'bicycle' insignia of the 16th/5th on the turret face above the righthand smoke grenade dischargers), threads its way through a coconut grove during a patrol with 1st Battalion, The Light Infantry, in 1992. (Soldier Magazine)

Europe (ACE) Mobile Force (Land) to protect the southern NATO flank. Formed into '4-car' troops of Scorpions and Scimitars with Striker ATGW in support, CVR(T) acted as the reconnaissance squadron for AMF(L) whose insignia is carried on the hull front and gunner's night cowl. Due to political reasons, the AMF exercise to be held in Turkey in 1990 was cancelled, as a result this Scorpion of 13th/18th Hussars was deployed.

Plate E1: *Spartan MCT, Mobile Milan Section, 1st Battalion, The Staffordshire Regiment, Operation 'Granby', Saudi Arabia, December 1990*

In British Army service, the Spartan equipped with Milan Compact Turret is known as MCT(S). This vehicle of the 1 STAFFORDS Mobile Milan

With a Union Flag flying at the radio antenna, the troop leader's Scimitar of 1 Troop, A Squadron, 16th/5th The Queen's Royal Lancers, speeds across the desert at the conclusion of Operation 'Desert Sabre'. Because of the open terrain, the traditional methods of

Medium Reconnaissance by stealth were inappropriate in the Gulf and CVR(T) vehicles often found themselves being outstripped by the formations they served; not necessarily because they were slower but because the advance was so rapid. (Alvis)

A Spartan of Support Troop, 'A' Squadron, 1st The Queen's Dragoon Guards, kicks up the sand as it thunders across the desert soon after the cessation of hostilities in the Gulf. Reminiscent of the squadron's advance at the head of 7th Armoured Brigade in the race to cut

the Kuwait/Basra road before the ceasefire was declared at 0800 on 28 February 1991, this Spartan displays the inverted black chevron of the Coalition Forces, the Chieftain stowage bins and rolls of CARM, typical of CVR(T) in the Gulf campaign of 1990-91. (Robin Watt)

Section is depicted at Al Fadili on 23 December 1990 during the training and work-up period prior to Operation 'Desert Sabre'. Four One Bravo is the callsign of the Troop Corporal's vehicle and it achieved notable success on G+2 (26 February 1991) when its commander, Corporal Darren 'Eddy' Fern, scored a 'left and right' (one hit with each missile) against a BMP and a T55. Finished in overall sand yellow, this vehicle carries the callsign 41B on each hull side and to the left of the rear hull door where a Union Flag is also displayed. Above the rear door is the legend TANK BUSTERS while along the top front face of the commander's sight is the name MAVERICK in black capital letters. The famous 'Red Jerboa' of 7th Armoured Brigade is painted on each hull side. On the side of the missile turret is the unit insignia adopted by 1 STAFFORDS in the Gulf which shows the 'Stafford Knot' upon a palm tree (a variation on the World War 2 insignia of the Afrika Korps).

Plate E2: *FV103 Spartan, Regimental Headquarters, 16th/5th The Queen's Royal Lancers, Operation 'Desert Sabre', Iraq, February 1991*

During Operation 'Desert Sabre', Lieutenant-Colonel Philip Scott, Commanding Officer of the 16th/5th, employed a Spartan as a 'battlefield taxi' to command and move between his far-flung reconnaissance elements. For security reasons, the vehicle carried no registration numbers or call sign but was readily discernible at close range as the CO's by the marking beside the driver's position of THE BOSS!. In its function as a command vehicle, it had a special radio fit, with three antennae. Accordingly, space was at a premium because, at times, up to six people were crammed inside, including the CO; radio operator; operations officers; intelligence officer; driver and an attached USAF Forward Air Controller who normally travelled in a Humvee; HMMWV (High Mobility Multi-purpose Wheeled Vehicle).

Accordingly there was a large amount of external stowage with a Chieftain bin above the rear door and a large stowage rack on top crammed with stores; the latter was covered with a sheet of CARM (Chemical Agent Resistant Material) painted with a rear facing black chevron, the mutual recognition marking of the Coalition Forces. This chevron was repeated on the hull sides; right rear stowage bin and lower hull front. Across the hull front is an inter-vehicle starting cable and immediately to the right of the driver, Corporal Bob 'Beano' Beadsmoore, is an upturned length of exhaust shroud grill acting as a tray for his personal kit, including a Sterling SMG and a red and yellow soft toy, 'Roy the Rooster', sent to the regiment by school children from its Midlands recruiting area. Above the vehicle commander's sight is a Trimble 'Trimpack' Global Position Satellite navigation aid, held down by bungees on a block of foam for want of a proper mounting bracket. Bolted to the front of the stowage basket behind the radio operator's hatch is a light grey BV (Boiling Vessel) so that constant cups of tea could be brewed for the command staff in the rear compartment. Another Chieftain bin is attached

As with Medium Reconnaissance, the doctrine of Close Reconnaissance for the mechanised infantry battalions and armoured regiments was radically modified in the Gulf. For Operation 'Desert Sabre', 1st Battalion, The Staffordshire Regiment, formed a powerful 'Recce Group' comprising the eight Scimitars of the Reconnaissance Platoon; the four MCTs of the Mobile Milan Section; a

REME Samson and an attached Forward Observation Officer in a Warrior. Capable of independent action if necessary, its primary task was flank protection of the Staffords Battlegroup and at times it acted in this role for 1st (UK) Armoured Division. Here, Callsign Two One, the Scimitar of the Recce Group commander, halts during a patrol some days after the ceasefire. (Richard Wootten)

along the RHS of the top stowage basket (as viewed from rear) while wired to the left hand hull side are 10 tracklinks; carried by each vehicle within a troop so that there were sufficient to make one complete track in case of mine damage. Above the rear hull compartment is a cerise air recognition panel. Below the rear door is the convoy distance marker. On the front right and rear left dustguard is painted the unit recognition code 3/1/HQ, particular to British Army vehicles during Operation 'Desert Sabre'.

Beside the British and Belgian Armies, a further 15 countries have purchased Scorpion and CVR(T) variants and sales continue of the Stormer family of vehicle. As of July 1994, 3738 CVR(T) and Stormer vehicles have been produced and foreign customers include: the Sultan of Brunei's Land Forces; Iran, Ireland, Malaysia, New Zealand, Nigeria, Oman , the Phillipines, Spain , Tanzania, Togo, United Arab Emirates and Venezuela. Note the later version towing bracket fitted at the rear; the four-cup smoke dischargers; different radio antennae and the base of the M63 anti-aircraft mount on the turret roof for a .50 calibre (12.7mm) M2 HB MG. (Irish Defence Forces)

Plate F: *FV102 Striker, Guided Weapons Troop, 'A' Squadron, 1st The Queen's Dragoon Guards, Objective Lead, Operation 'Desert Sabre', 26 February 1991*

'A' Squadron, QDG, was the original reconnaissance unit deployed with 7th Armoured Brigade. With the formation of 1st (BR) Armoured Division it came under operational control of 16th/5th, The Queen's Royal Lancers, but it continued to operate independently on occasions and eventually reverted to 7th Armoured Brigade at the conclusion of the campaign. Reflecting this allegiance, the Striker carries the Red Jerboa on each hull side together with the Red Dragon of Wales showing the regiment's provenance as 'The Welsh Cavalry'. The vehicle's registration number 07FF68 is painted on the lower hull front and to the left of the rear door with the convoy distance

The author tries his hand in the latest addition to the CVR(T) range, the Sabre, at the Alvis Customer Training School. This view shows many of the modifications made to combine the Fox turret and Scorpion hull including the adaptor ring to accommodate the smaller turret diameter ring of Fox; the co-axial L94A1 Chain Gun and its spare barrel stowage tube on top of the bin on the left side of the turret; a new domed hatch for the gunner; modified turret bins with quick release mechanisms; additional rear hull and side bins as well as new stowage bins across the front of the hull for 'trackbashing' tools; revised highlights and light clusters; new smoke dischargers and a higher gun crutch to allow the driver improved vision to his right-hand side when driving 'head-out' with the 30mm Rarden in its crutch. The first regiment to be equipped with Sabre is to be the Queen's Own Yeomanry followed by 9th/12th Royal Lancers; each receiving 48 Sabres. (Simon Dunstan)

A Scorpion of the Reconnaissance Troop of 1st Royal Tank Regiment (RTR) carries the distinctive 'Chinese Eyes' of the Fourth following the amalgamation of the two regiments; other markings include the 'Fear Naught' insignia of the RTR and along the side bin the name Robertson VC, a Tank Corps Victoria Cross winner in the Great War. The vehicle is shown in the final Scorpion configuration before its withdrawal from service in 1994. (Simon Dunstan)

marker below the latter. Mutual recognition markings of the inverted black chevron are displayed on all quarters and it carries a yellow air recognition panel above the missile launcher bins. On the extreme left hand missile launcher bin door is the A Squadron insignia stencilled in red above which is a black plate bearing the callsign Three One within a triangle with the letter A to the top right indicating the Troop Sergeant's vehicle within the GW Troop. On the right hand hull side is a Chieftain long bin. Note behind the commander's cupola is the egg-shaped receiver of the GPS navigation aid - a device that proved to be of crucial importance to the Coalition victory. Of interest, the vehicles of 'A' Squadron, QDG, did not carry a unit recognition code during Operation 'Desert Sabre'.

Plate G1: *FV107, Scimitar, 2 Troop, 'B' Squadron, The Light Dragoons, Operation 'Grapple', Bosnia, August 1993*

This Scimitar of The Light Dragoons is shown during checkpoint duty at a Muslim/Serb confrontation line in the town of Turbe in Central Bosnia on 29 August 1993. The vehicle is finished in overall white as are all vehicles of the United Nations Protection Force (UNPROFOR) in the

former Republic of Yugoslavia. Based at Vitez at this date, the Scimitars of 'B' Squadron carry prominent UN markings on each side turret bin; the rear turret bin and on the lower hull front below the registration number; the subject vehicle being 00GH05 which is repeated on the rear hull plate to the right of the convoy distance marker as viewed from the rear. From the same viewpoint, the markings on the turret rear bin are as follows; bottom left a Union Flag sticker above which is the UN vehicle registration number UNPF 41331 painted in black on a white plate with a black border; at top right are the letters UN and below is the vehicle callsign Two One, denoting Second Troop Sergeant, beside the stencilled 'B' Squadron insignia; all these markings being painted in black on the white base colour. On the left hand radio antenna is the white and blue United Nations flag while on the other is the Union Flag; British vehicles are now discouraged from displaying national flags and the regimental pennant is normally flown instead. Most Scimitars of The Light Dragoons carry their impressive regimental cap badge insignia on the armoured cowl of the gunner's night sight (see scrap view and photographs in text) but this Scimitar carries the standard yellow warning plate inscribed with black

Laden with spares and stores, a Samson of 13th/18th Royal Hussars waits by the roadside during Exercise 'Highwayman' on Salisbury Plain in February 1989. The hull of the Samson is similar to that used for the Spartan with a heavy-duty winch fitted inside the hull on the right side with the two crew seats, one for the vehicle commander and the other for a fitter being on the left side. It is also highly effective for river crossings where the addition of an appliqué propeller kit and its ability for self-recovery, allows Samson to negotiate virtually any river or inland waterway. (Tim Neate)

ammunition boxes with a short length of mesh grill between them to create additional stowage space; on the right hand box as viewed is another UN registration number plate – UNPF 41331. The Latin inscription reads 'It Flourishes Forever' (motto of the 13th/18th) and 'We Shall Be Worthy' (motto of the 15th/19th).

Plate G2: *FV107 Scimitar, Reconnaissance squadron, Para-Commando Brigade, Belgian UN Contingent, Somalia, August 1993*
As part of the Belgian Army's strategic reserve, the Para-Commando Brigade is assigned to the Forces d'Intervention and as Belgium's contribution to NATOs Rapid Reaction Corps. During 1993, elements of the Brigade formed part of the Belgian contingent to United Nations peacekeeping operations in Somalia. It included two reconnaissance squadrons, manned in turn by 3e Lanciers; 4e Chasseurs à Cheval; 1e Lanciers; 1e Jagers te Paard and the Para-Commando anti-tank

letters – DANGER KEEP CLEAR OF THIS DOOR; a curious addition to an Armoured Fighting Vehicle in a war zone but required by Health and Safety regulations. Typical of all CVR(T) on operations, this Scimitar has additional stowage bins and baskets including a Chieftain small bin attached to the right hand side of the rear turret bin; a Chieftain short bin beside the engine and, beside the driver, the angle iron and mesh grill stowage basket, characteristic of Scimitars in Bosnia. Across the front are two

company and comprised 26 Scimitars; eight Scorpions; nine Spartans; two Sultans; two Samaritans and three Samsons. This Scimitar is painted white overall as is standard for United Nations peacekeeping forces. On the front hull plate is the insignia of the Para-Commando Brigade beside the Belgian national tricolor in the centre below which is the vehicle registration number 65263 preceded by a narrow tricolor. This plate is repeated on the lower rear hull. Draped over the gun mantlet and the cowl of the gunner's night sight is a red air recognition panel while on the face of the cowl is the same warning plate as in Plate G1. Close to hand, each crew member has an FN-FNC 5.56mm Assault Rifle. The Scimitars and Spartans of the Belgian Army deployed to Gregoire Kayibanda International Airport at Kigali in Rwanda carried large black UN markings on the turret sides and centrally on the rear bin.

A troop of Strikers of 13th/18th Royal Hussars hurry up and wait during Exercise 'Highwayman' in February 1989; in place of natural vegetation for camouflage these vehicles show the modern practice of scrim netting and hessian strips to break up their outline. Striker is based on the hull of the Spartan APC with five BAe Swingfire missiles in armoured launcher bins at the rear of the hull. Once the five Swingfire missiles in the launcher bins have been fired, one of the crew members has to leave the vehicle to reload them with another five missiles which are stowed under armour in the rear hull giving a total of 10 missiles carried, although during the Gulf War additional missiles were crammed inside. (Tim Neate)

INDEX

Figures in **bold** refer to illustrations.